This book belongs to:

_____

_____

the

the the the
the the the

of

of of of of
of of of of

and

and   and   and

and   and   and

a

a   a   a   a

a   a   a   a

to

to   to   to   to

to   to   to   to

in

in in in in in

in in in in in

is

is is is is is is

is is is is is is

you

you you you

you you you

that

that that that

that that that

it

it it it it

it it it it

he

he he he he

he he he he

was

was was was

was was was

for

for for for

for for for

on

on on on on

on on on on

are

are are are

are are are

as

as as as as

as as as as

with

with with with

with with with

his

his his his his

his his his his

they

they they they

they they they

I

I I I I I

I I I I I

at

at   at   at   at

at   at   at   at

be

be   be   be   be

be   be   be   be

this

this this this

this this this

have

have have

have have

from

from from from

from from from

or

or or or or

or or or or

one

one one one

one one one

had

had had had

had had had

by

by by by by

by by by by

words

words words

words words

but

but but but but

but but but but

not

not not not

not not not

what

what what what

what what what

all

all all all all

all all all all

were

were were were

were were were

we

we we we we

we we we we

when

when when when
when when when

your

your your your
your your your

can

can can can

can can can

said

said said said

said said said

there

there there there

there there there

use

use use use

use use use

an

an an an an

an an an an

each

each each each

each each each

which

which which which

which which which

she

she she she she

she she she she

do

do do do do

do do do do

how

how how how

how how how

FUN ACTIVITIES!

TRACING LETTERS

Aa   Bb   Cc   Dd

Ee   Ff   Gg   Hh

Ii   Jj   Kk   Ll

Mm   Nn   Oo   Pp

Qq   Rr   Ss   Tt

Uu   Vv   Ww   Xx

Yy   Zz

MATCH & TRACE

Draw a line from the picture to the letter it starts with. Then, trace the letters.

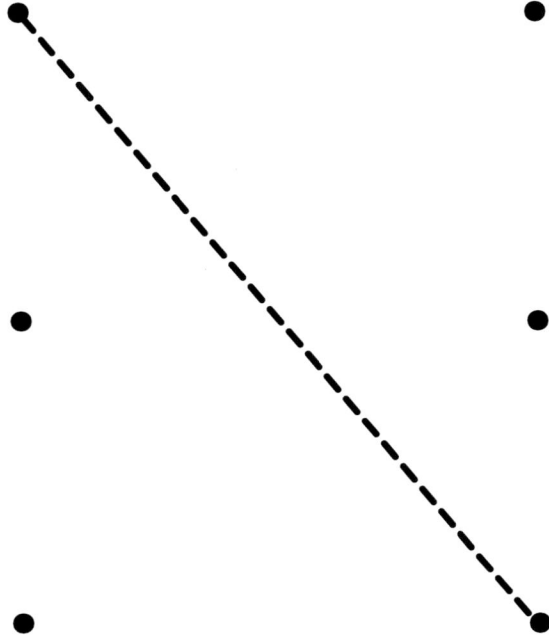

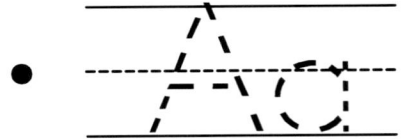

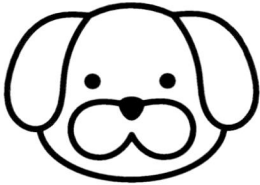

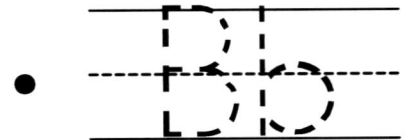

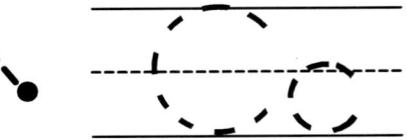

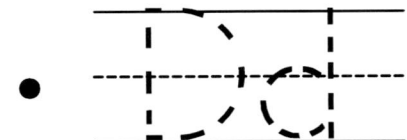

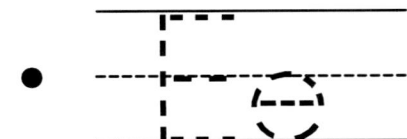

Aa

Bb

Cc

Dd

Ee

MATCH & TRACE

 • •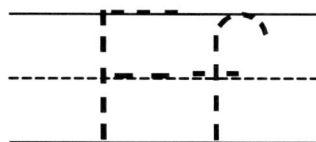

 • •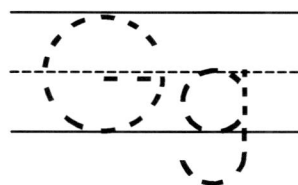

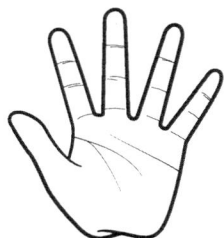 • •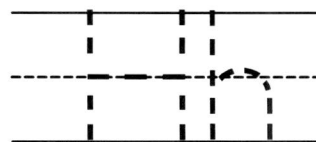

 • •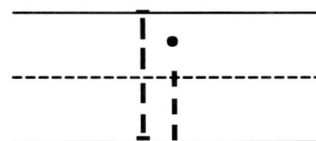

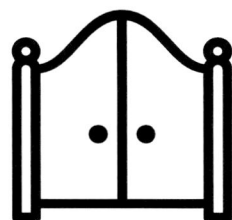 • •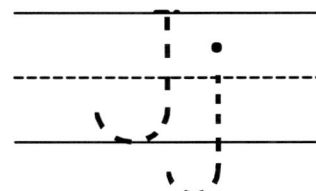

MATCH & TRACE

   •   •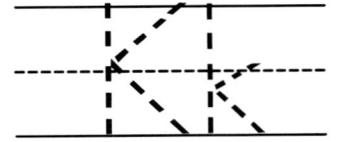

   •   •

   •   •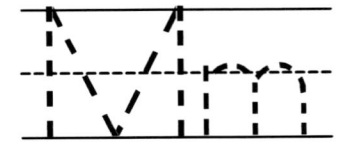

   •   •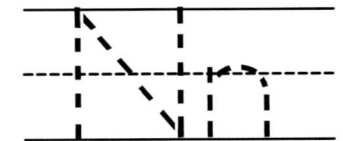

   •   •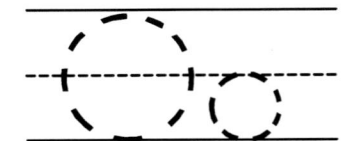

MATCH & TRACE

 • •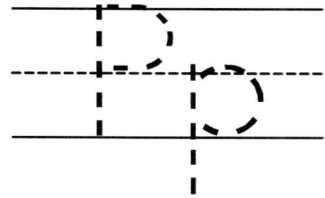

 • •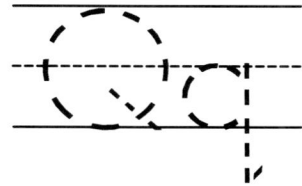

 • •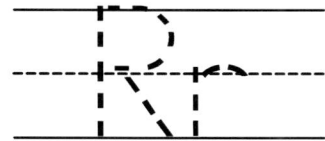

 • •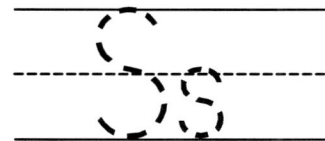

 • •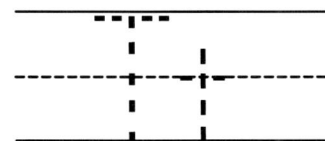

MATCH & TRACE

   •   •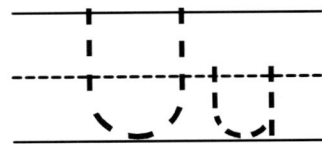

   •   •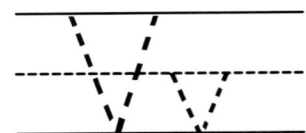

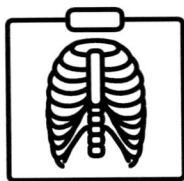   •   •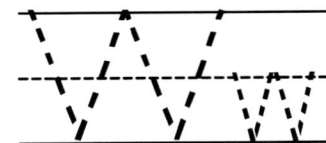

   •   •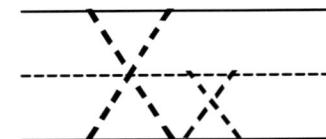

   •   •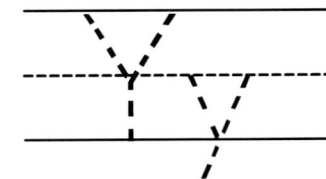

   •   •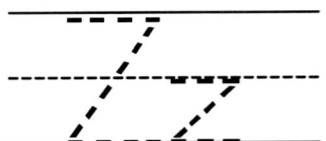

Farm Animals

Fill in the missing letters

D _ N _ EY

D _ CK

GO _ T

G _ OS _

D _ G

H _ N

Farm Animals

Fill in the missing letters

H _ R _ E

B _ _

PI _

C _ T

M _ U _ E

RA _ B _ T

THE END

Made in the USA
Las Vegas, NV
05 August 2021